This book belongs to

_____

_____

This picture book is dedicated to my mother, who introduced me to the great Persian books, Bustan and Gulistan, by Saadi Sherazi.

Dear Reader,

This story is inspired by the wise teachings of Saadi Shirazi, shared here in a way that's easy and fun for young readers.

Saadi Shirazi was a wonderful Persian poet and storyteller from the 13th century, famous for his wise words and inspiring tales. His book, Bustan (The Orchard), is full of stories that teach us important lessons about being kind, honest, and brave. Bustan is considered one of the greatest books of all time!

The purpose of this picture book, based on one of Saadi's stories from Bustan, is to introduce his wonderful work to young readers, so that as they grow, they can enjoy and learn from Saadi's wise teachings even more.

As you read this book, may you feel love, kindness, and compassion and enjoy learning from Saadi's wonderful teachings!

With warm wishes,
Rooma Para

The Lion and the Fox

Picture book based on a story by

Saadi Shirazi

Created by

Rooma Para

In a small village next to a big, green jungle, there lived a young boy named Rob.

Rob loved to play and have fun all day. He would much rather run around, chase butterflies, and climb trees than do any work.

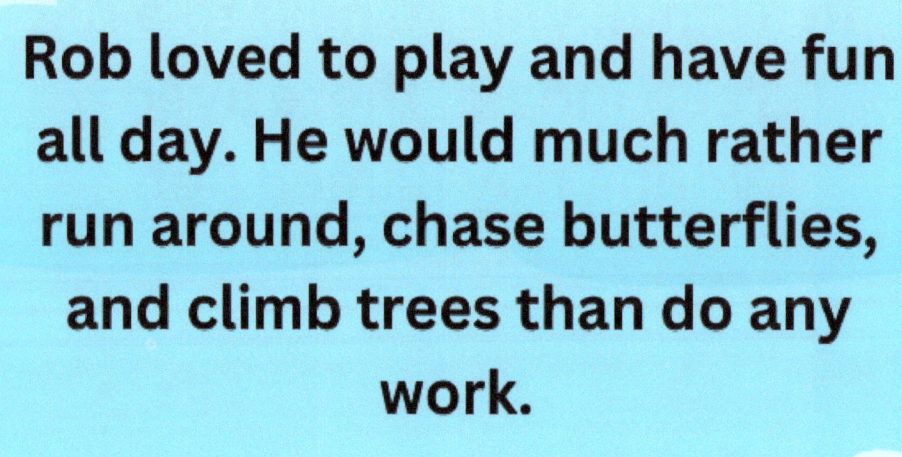

Like every child in the village, Rob had to help with the chores at home. He was asked to gather firewood for the family and sometimes look for fruits. He didn't like this at all and would often complain.

He would always grumble about how tired he was and how unfair it seemed.

Deep down, Rob dreamed he could just sit and have everything he needed come to him without doing any work.

One morning, Rob wandered into the jungle in search of firewood.

Although the jungle was beautiful, it could also be dangerous, and Rob knew he had to be careful.

As he was searching for dry branches, he spotted something strange behind a thick bush.

His curiosity took over, and he moved closer. To his surprise, there lay a fox.

The fox was weak. It couldn't walk.

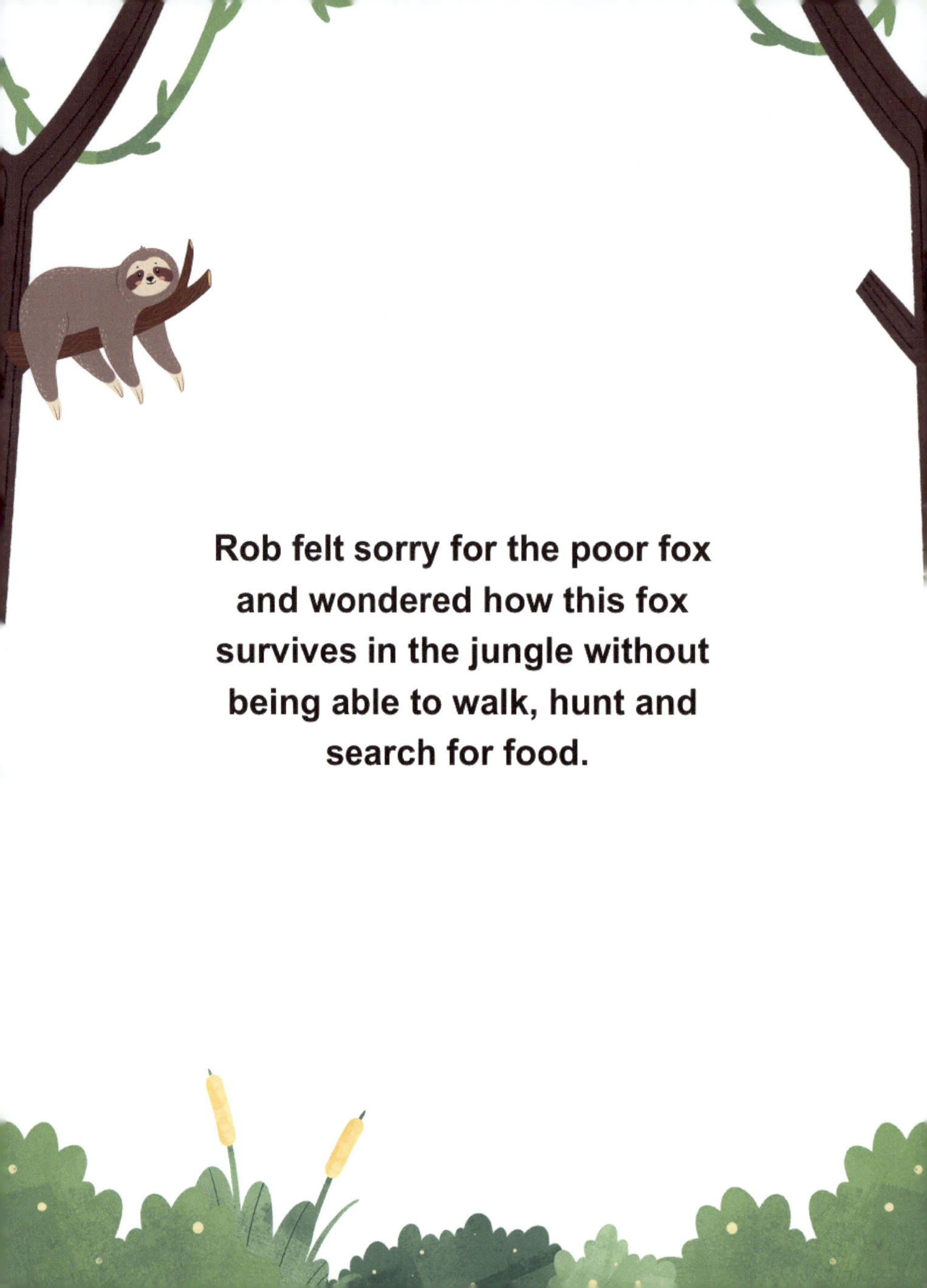

Rob felt sorry for the poor fox and wondered how this fox survives in the jungle without being able to walk, hunt and search for food.

He quickly climbed up a tree, going as high as he could so no one could see him, but he could still peek out to see what was coming. His eyes got big with fear.

A huge lion emerged from the trees, its golden fur glowing in the sunlight.

The lion came carrying fresh meat, its lunch! Rob's heart was racing. He watched from his hiding place as the lion walked straight toward the fox!

But something surprising happened. The lion didn't harm the fox at all. Instead, it sat down next to the fox.

The lion started to eat its food. Rob was amazed to see why wasn't the lion chasing the fox away or trying to eat it?

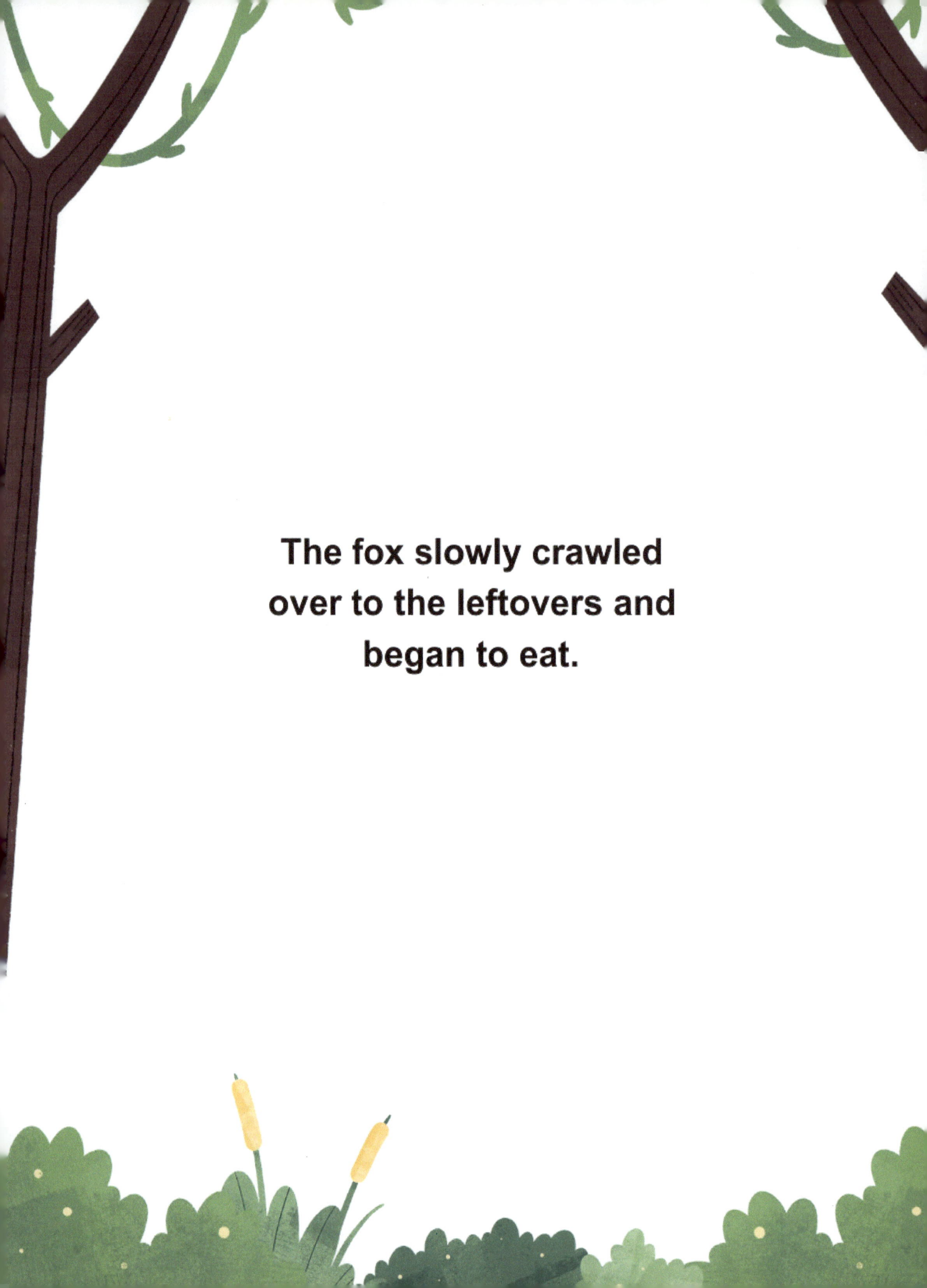

The fox slowly crawled over to the leftovers and began to eat.

Rob couldn't believe his eyes. The fox, unable to hunt, was still able to eat because of the lion's leftovers.

But he wasn't completely sure it would happen again. He shook his head in disbelief, thinking it must have been a coincidence.

BURP!

The next day, curious to see if the lion would return, Rob decided to visit the same spot in the jungle.

He hid behind the same tree and waited. Hours passed, and just when he thought nothing would happen, the bushes rustled once more. Out stepped the lion with food, just like the day before.

Again, it sat beside the fox, ate until it was full, and left the rest for the fox and walked away.

The fox ate happily once more.

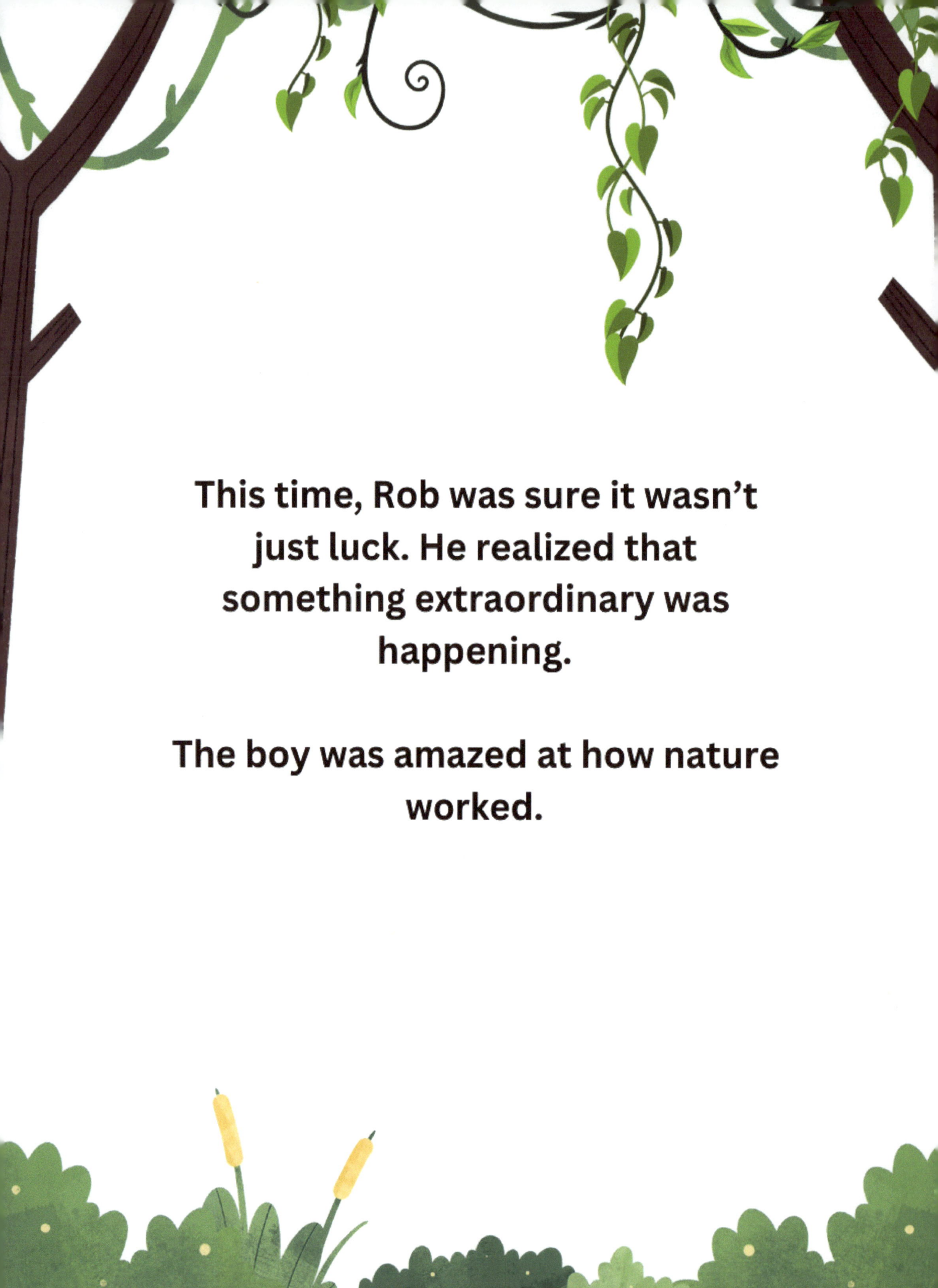

This time, Rob was sure it wasn't just luck. He realized that something extraordinary was happening.

The boy was amazed at how nature worked.

After witnessing this event,
Rob had an idea.

He decided that from now on,
he would stop working hard to
find food for himself. If the
fox could live by waiting for
food to come to it, surely he
could too.

The next morning, instead of gathering wood or searching for fruits, Rob found a quiet corner under a shady tree and sat down.

He didn't even tell his family. He just waited, believing that, like the fox, his meal would come to him.

He waited. Hours passed. He felt hungry but he told himself to be patient.

As the sun moved across the sky, Rob's hunger grew, his stomach began to rumble.

Night fell, but nothing happened.

No lion came to bring him food, and no one else did either.

Rob reached a stage where he had no strength left in his body.

He started crying and just when he was about to pass out, a gentle voice spoke to him.

The boy suddenly understood. He realized that he made a mistake.

He realized that waiting and doing nothing wasn't the answer.

The fox had no choice. It was disabled and weak. It couldn't walk and hunt. But Rob was healthy, young, and capable.

Suddenly, everything made sense. He realized that he ought to be strong like the lion, take care of himself and help those in need.

From that day on, Rob changed his ways. He worked hard to complete his chores, but now he did it with joy in his heart.

Rob never forgot the lesson of the fox and the lion. He became known in his village as a strong and kind young boy, always willing to lend a hand and help others, just as the lion had helped the fox.

Human beings are members of a whole,
In creation of one essence and soul.
If one member is afflicted with pain,
Other members uneasy will remain.
If you have no sympathy for human pain,
The name of human you cannot retain.

By
Saadi Shirazi

A beautifully created picture book that brings to life the timeless wisdom and teachings of Saadi Shirazi for young readers.

Copyright © Rooma Para, 2024. All rights reserved.

No part of this book may be reproduced, stored in a retrieval system, or transmitted in any form or by any means, including mechanical, electronic, photocopying, recording, or otherwise, without the prior written of the publisher

Title: The Lion and the Fox: Picture Book based on a story by Saadi Shirazi
First Paperback edition Nov 2024
ISBN: 978-1-0691336-2-5 (Paperback)
ISBN: 978-1-0691336-0-1 (Hardcover Book)
ISBN: 978-1-0691336-1-8 (eBook)

Based on a story from Bustan (The Orchard) by the 13th century Persian poet Saadi Shirazi
Book designed/ created on Canva.com by Rooma Para
Author Rooma Para

Every effort has been made to trace or contact all copyright holders. This is self-published book and publisher will be pleased to make any omissions or rectify any mistakes brought to their attention at the earliest opportunity.

www.ingramcontent.com/pod-product-compliance
Lightning Source LLC
Chambersburg PA
CBHW040100160426
43193CB00002B/25